I0481304

OPTIONS TRADING

The Basics of Options Trading for Beginners and the Best Simplified Strategies to Make Money

Table of Contents

INTRODUCTION

Congratulations on downloading this book and thank you for doing so.

The following chapters will discuss everything that you need to know in order to get started with options trading. Options are a bit different compared to other forms of investments. They allow the investor the right, but not the obligation, to purchase an asset at a later time. If things go well, the investor is able to purchase that asset, usually at a discounted price, and they can then make money from this purchase. If things go poorly, the investor does not have to purchase the asset, but they will lose their initial deposit. This guidebook will go more in-depth about options and how you can get started on them while making money in the process.

In this guidebook, we will not only discuss some of the basics of options trading, but also why options are a good investment choice, how to get started with trading options, some successful trading strategies you can use, common mistakes that many traders will make, and some of the steps that you can take to reduce your risks with options trading.

When you are ready to expand out your portfolio, or at least get started with investing in the first place, then make sure to read through this guidebook to help you get started in options trading.

There are plenty of books on this subject on the market, thanks again for choosing this one! Every effort was made to ensure it is full of as much useful information as possible, please enjoy!

CHAPTER 1

THE BASICS OF OPTIONS TRADING

When it comes to finding a good investment opportunity, one that will not cost you a lot of money to get started with but can make a large profit, then it is time to take a look at investments. There are many parts that come with options trading and you need to do your research ahead of time, although anyone can join this market and make a profit. Let's take a closer look at these options and how you can get started making money in no time.

What are options?

The first thing that we need to look at is what options are. For an experienced investor, you will be able to see that they have a lot of different types of investments in their portfolio. They don't just work with stocks or their retirement account. Instead, they may have real estate, business investments, stocks, bonds, mutual funds, and more. Some of these portfolios are also going to include options, but this is not as common as some of the other choices.

An option is a contract that will give you the authority, but not the obligation, to purchase or sell an asset or security in the future. You may do this in order to get the asset at a discount later on if things are about to change. For example, a land developer may choose to enter an option with a landowner to purchase some plots within the next few years. The land developer may do this because the city is about to pass a few new regulations that would allow the value of land to go up. If these are passed, the land developer would be able to purchase the land at the agreed price, regardless of how much the market value of that land went up.

However, if the regulations do not go through, the land developer does not need to purchase the land. They will lose their initial deposit, but they won't have to purchase the land that they likely don't want now.

With options, you will pay a certain cost and this will last for a certain amount of time. Some options will last for a few months and others may last for a few years. You will know the length of the option before you enter into the agreement and you can exercise the right to purchase at any time during that period. So, if the option is for two years, you could decide to purchase at a year if you would like.

The call and put options

As an investor, there are two main things that you can do with your investment including a call and a put option. The call option is often going to be used similar to a deposit for doing something in the future. Let's go back to the example of the land developer. You may want the option to purchase a lot later on in the future, but you only want to use this right if the city passes certain laws. To do this, the developer would purchase their call option from the landowner. The landowner and developer would put in the price that the developer will pay for the land if they exercise their rights in the next three years, and then the developer will need to put down a deposit.

This deposit is to help provide an incentive to the landowner to agree to the option. If the market price goes up in the next three years, why would the owner want to take on option rather than put the land up for sale and taking the best price? The developer will offer them a deposit of the call option. If the developer decides to purchase the land, then the deposit will go towards the amount that they owe. If the developer decides to not purchase the land, then the owner would get to keep the deposit. Either way, the landowner would get something for agreeing to the option.

There is also something that is known as a put option. When you are investing, this is like an insurance policy that will help to keep your portfolio nice and safe. Let's say that an investor has a big portfolio, with many stocks and other investments. But as they are looking at the economy, they become worried that there will be a recession and their portfolio may end up losing some value. As an investor, they want to protect their portfolio as much as possible and the put-call will be able to help with this.

Let's say that the S&P 500 is trading at 2500. The investor would then be able to choose a put option that then allows them to sell their portfolio at 2500 at any time during the next two years (or a different time frame based on what they have with their put option). If at any time during the next two years, the market crashes by twenty percent or more, which is 500 points inside the portfolio, the investor is safe. They would be able to sell at 2250 rather than 2000 that the market values the portfolio. It does result in a loss for the investor, but the loss is much less than what others may be facing.

Of course, there is going to be a premium, or a cost, for exercising this option. If the investor is wrong and the market doesn't end up dropping during this time period, the investor will lose the premium that they paid upfront.

Going through these examples shows you a few key points about options. The first is that whenever you purchase an option, it provides you with the right, but not the obligation, to do something with it. You can either exercise this right, or you can let the expiration date go by and not purchase the option. However, if you let the expiration date go by, you will lose your premium, so you do have some risk involved.

The second thing is that the option is just going to be a contract that will deal with the specific asset that you want to purchase or protect. You will not actually own the asset when you purchase an option, at least not right away. Sometimes this is going to work out well for you, and other times it may not, but a smart investor will be able to make decent predictions that will provide them with a good profit from these options.

How do options work?

If you have worked with other types of investments in the past, you may notice that options are going to work differently. Options contracts are like price probabilities for events that may happen in the future. An investor is going to see if an event is likely to occur before purchasing the option. The more likely an event is to happen, the more expensive the option will be. Understanding how the options process works can help you to pick out good options that will make you a profit.

Let's take a look at an example of how this could work by using a call option with IBM. The strike price is going to be $200 with IBM currently trading at $127 and the options are going to expire in three months. Remember, the call option is going to give you the right (although you won't be obligated), to purchase shares of IBM at $200 anytime during the next three months.

With this option, if the stock prices of IBM end up going above $200, you will win. It doesn't matter that we aren't sure of the price for this particular option right now. What we do know is that this option, if it expires in one month rather than three months, will end up costing less because the chances of anything occurring during this smaller interval of time is going to be smaller. On the other hand, if this same option lasts for the next year, it is going to cost you more because it is more likely that the stock price will go up to $200 or higher sometime during that year.

Now, let's look at what happens when you bring back the three-month expiration that we had in the beginning. Another thing that can help you increase your odds of getting a profit is if the price of this stock gets close to

$200. In fact, the closer that the stock price is to this at the beginning then the more likely you will see this event happen.

As the price of the asset begins to rise, the gap between your asset price and the strike price will widen. When this happens, you will notice that the cost of the option will be less. So, if you set your strike price at $190 rather than $200, the cost of this option is going to be higher because it is much more likely that the stock will reach $190 instead of the $200. However, if you set a strike price or $230, the price of the option will cost less because this is much less likely to happen.

Why would I work with options?

Working in options can be really profitable. You get the chance to work in the market without actually having to purchase the underlying asset, and it can provide you with a huge profit in the process. In addition, you can choose whether to actually purchase the asset at the expiration date (or before) or to leave it alone. There is some risk in this because if you don't purchase the asset, you lose the deposit, but it is much better than losing out like you can in the stock market.

For example, to purchase the asset, you may need to come up with $100,00. But with an options contract, you can put a $3,000 down payment on it. If the asset price goes up and you will make a profit, you can sell the option for the higher amount and make a profit. If the market goes down and the asset is worth less, later on, you don't lose the $100,000 (or however much it goes down on the market). You would only lose $3,000.

Many beginners like to work with options because they have this leverage. They can work with assets that cost a lot more than what they have in their account. They can get all the profits that come with that, but not as much risk as leveraging other choices. When you add this to the fact that you get a lot of assets to choose from, the fact that you can make money whether the market is going up or down and that options are easy to work with, and you can see why many people choose to add options to their portfolio.

Working with options can be a great way for you to make a profit in the stock market without actually having to own anything in the process. You basically purchase the right, but not the obligation, to purchase an asset sometime in the future. If things work well for you and the asset is worth later in the future, you would exercise your right for the purchase. But if things go south, you would only lose your deposit by not investing. It takes some time to work with options and to get used to the market, but options can be a great way to increase your portfolio and make a good profit in the process.

CHAPTER 2

WHY ARE OPTIONS A GOOD CHOICE FOR INVESTING?

As we mentioned in the last chapter, there are a lot of different investment opportunities that you can choose from. Options are a good choice because they can help to increase your profits, or at least limit your losses, depending on what option you decide to use. There are many great benefits that come with using options, which is why they have become so popular to use. Some of the benefits that you will get from using options include:

- Options are flexible: When you are working with options, you get a ton of flexibility. You can choose whether you will purchase or sell the option when the expiration date comes. You can pick out the expiration date you want to work with. You can pick from many different strategies and even assets that you invest in. You even get the choice of your strike price. Depending on the option that you work with, you can even earn a profit when the market goes down. Some people find all this flexibility complicated, but if you know how options work, you will enjoy this flexibility and how it helps you make an income.

- Smaller entry amounts: Sometimes it is hard to get into the stock market without having a lot of money. Stocks are expensive, but you will find that stock options can be cheap. With options, you can make a ton of money with only $1,000, something that you are not able to do with the stock market. In addition, if you don't have to put as much capital down on the investment, you won't have as much money to lose.

- Gain leverage: Having leverage can be a good advantage when you are investing. Inside options trading, you can gain leverage because you give yourself some additional choices compared to what is available with the stock market for the same price. In addition, you will get a fair amount of returns when you are working with options, so this is another positive to working with options.

- Lower risk: You will find that there are plenty of options that are low-risk. These risks are often more affordable, which is the main reason that it helps to limit the risk that you take. In addition, you can use many of the strategies that we will discuss in this guidebook to reduce the risk even more. As a beginner in options, you should stick with some of the less risky options to help you learn the market before moving on to the harder options.

- More benefits compared to working with the stock market: Most people who would like to invest will choose to work with stock trading. But going with options can provide you with more benefits. To start, options trading is usually more profitable compared to the stock market. Dealing with a small movement inside the stock market will end up affecting the option you hold quite a bit more. For example, the stock market may only move one percent, while the option would end up moving ten percent. If you are good at picking options and making good decisions, this can result in a lot more profit for the investor. In addition, for you to make money in the stock market the stock needs to go up. With options, you have the possibility of making money whether the option goes up, down, or doesn't move at all.

In some cases, beginners are going to find that options are tricky to work with. They are different than some of the other investments that you may have worked with in the past and this can make them more difficult to work with. However, there are quite a few benefits to working with options, which makes them perfect for earning a good profit in the process.

CHAPTER 3

THE PROCESS OF TRADING OPTIONS

Now that you know a little bit more about options and some of the benefits of choosing options trading, it is time to learn more about how to get started with trading in options. This does not have to be a complicated process and this chapter is going to break down the steps to make it easier for the beginner to get started. As a beginner, you may be worried that it is going to be too difficult to get into options, but with the right information, and the right people beside you to help, you will do great with options.

Getting ready

Before you jump in with options trading, there are a few steps that you must complete in order to be successful.

Do your research to find out the basics about options, such as a good price for options and the types that are available. As a beginner, the more information that you can find about options, the more prepared you will be to find success.

Once you are pretty certain that you have a good grasp on trading and what comes with options, it is a good idea to think about why you want to go into trading? How much money would you like to make and what other goals are important to you during this time? It is always a good idea to be precise in your goals because you can develop your strategy around this. It also helps to break frustration and overspending from the start.

But the most important thing that you can do in this first step is to make sure that you create what is known as a trading plan. This is basically a plan that lists out everything that you want to accomplish such as your expectations, goals, and the guidelines that you will follow with your strategy. Those who don't go into this with a plan are the ones who add a lot of risk to the whole process.

Picking out your broker

Once your research is done and you have made a few important decisions about options trading, it is time to pick out a broker. Some investors decide to forgo having a broker because it saves them money. It is up to you whether a broker is important or not, but if you are new to investing, you will find that a broker can definitely be worth the money.

When you are working with a broker, you will need to pay them some commission or fee for the work that they do. The amount you pay will depend on the broker you are working with and how much help you need. If you just want to use their platform and ask a few questions, it will cost you a lot less than if you need someone to do the trades for you and walk you through the process.

When you begin working with broker for the first time, they will most likely sit down with you. During this discussion, you will talk about how much risk you are willing to take, your financial history, and discuss some information about options. The broker will then be able to talk about your trading level, the level that you will stay with that keeps your risks at a safe level while still making a profit. This is one of the best places to start out so that you know a plan ahead of time and you and your broker are on the same page.

Choosing the underlying assets

Since the option is going to be a derivative of something else, meaning you are just signing a contract for an underlying asset rather than owning the asset, there are quite a few that you can pick from. You can purchase and sell options contracts on things like foreign currencies, bonds, stocks, and commodities. This is good news for the investor because it adds some more flexibility and you can work with the underlying asset that you are the most comfortable with.

Managing your risk and your money

The next thing that the investor should consider when they are ready, to begin with options trading is the process you will use in order to manage your money and the risks that you face. Like any investment, options can be risky and if you decide to trade without having a plan, you will end up losing your money on the trades. When you decide to create a trading plan for options, it needs to include, among other things, the amount of risk that you are willing to take on each trade.

It is a good idea to get this plan in place right away and then stick with it. When you create a plan like that, you are effectively keeping the emotions out of the game. As soon as emotions come into the game, it is time to give up trading altogether. Emotions lead you to make bad decisions, decisions that will lose a lot of money in the options market. Regardless of whether you are dealing with greed, excitement, worry, or something else, you will lose money in the options trading market when you make decisions with your emotions.

Before you ever enter the market or any decisions with trading, it is a good idea to take a deep breath, look over the trading plan that you created, and then make decisions that align with this plan.

Diversify

One thing that you should consider when you enter any type of investment, but especially with options trading, is how to diversify. This is a great way to limit your risks because it allows you to split up your money into various investments. When you put your money into one investment, you take on more risk. If that one investment does poorly, you end up losing all of your money in the process. But when you split up your money between a few investments, it is possible for one to do poorly, while another does well, and your money is not at risk as much.

Position Sizing

This may sound like a fancy step to go with, but it actually isn't that hard and can make a world of difference with how well your trade goes. All that position sizing means is that you are going to decide the amount of money, or how much capital you will use, that will be spent on a specific position while trading. This is sometimes compared to diversifying because it is not a good idea to spend all of your money in one position. It allows you to keep complete control over your capital.

You can even use this to control the losses that you suffer, protecting yourself against big losses even as a beginner.

Planning out your trades

At this point, it is time to plan out the trades that you want to do. You can choose to do this on your own or you can work with your broker depending on what you are the most comfortable with. When you are ready to plan out some of your trades, make sure to go through these steps:

- Forecasting: With this part, it is time to make predictions about what is going to happen in the market and with the asset that you want to work with. You will basically predict whether that asset is going to fall or rise in price over a specific amount of time. This forecast is going to help you pick out the best strategy to use and can even make it easier to pick out the right option.

- Setting goals: Here, you need to outline some goals that you want to work on. You can set your goals based on how much money you would like to make the trade and how long you want to remain in the trade. Having these goals not only help you to stay on track during the trade. They will also help you to figure out whether the trade was successful at the end.

- Choosing the right strategies: Later in this book, we will discuss some of the best strategies that you can use to help with options trading. There are many great ones, but it often depends on what you like working with and how the market is behaving. Before you talk to your broker about a trade, it is a good idea to pick out the strategy that you want to work with.

- Pick out the position sizing: For this step, you are going to decide how much money you want to place with each option. This will make it easier to see your risks before you get into the market, so you can decide if it is the right one for you.

Making the trades

After spending some time on the above steps, you now need to contact your broker and the two of you can work on placing the right orders so you can enter the options market. It is likely that you have already set up your funds through the broker, so getting the orders done quickly should not be an issue. You are now going to tell the broker how you would like to use those funds and which orders should be placed.

This is the point where you will enter into the trade. At this time, you should also write out what needs to happen for you to exit the trade. Do you plan to stay in the trade until your contracts expire? Will you end up closing them out early once you receive important information? Is there something else that will determine when you will exit the market? It is always a good idea to set out these conditions ahead of time. That way, you know what to look for without getting caught up in the market if something changes.

Monitoring your trades

After you have talked to your broker and placed your order, the trades will be completed. This does not mean that your work is done. It is not enough for the investor to put their money into the market and then ignore what is going on. If you want to ensure that you will make enough money in the market of options, then you will still need to spend some time monitoring your trades. You have to keep a close eye on all your options until the expiration date or until you decide to purchase the option.

There are a variety of things that you will need to do in order to monitor your trade. First, you must keep some good records of the trade so that you are always making good decisions regarding holding the option. You can then look through these records to figure out whether you should stay in the market or close out of it. You can also watch the market and figure out if your option is going the way that you would like. Your broker can help you to monitor the option and can give you advice on how to proceed with the market changes.

And that is all that you need to do in order to join the options market and to start earning money on this investment. If you work with a good broker, learn the process of trading in options, and pick out a good strategy, then you will earn a great return on investment without a ton of work. While there are some risks that come with every type of investment, options trading can be a safe and secure choice to make for every type of investor.

CHAPTER 4

SUCCESSFUL TRADING STRATEGIES

Now that you have learned a little bit about options trading and how to understand the market, it is time to move into some of the trading strategies that you can use. Everyone needs to have some kind of trading strategy in place to help them be successful with options. Jumping into the market and hoping things go well is not a good strategy to use. Your strategy is there to help you to know what market you are working in, how much you need to spend when to get into the market, and even when to exit the market.

The good news is there are a lot of different strategies that you can work with. These strategies will all work based on the market conditions around you and the options that you are interested in investing in. Let's take a look at some of the best trading strategies that you can pick from to help you get the best results.

Picking strategies based on the market

First, we are going to take a look at how you can pick out your strategy based on the market conditions around you. You are able to pick out options and make money no matter what kind of market you are working in as long as you pick out a good strategy. Let's look at a few different market situations and how you should handle them.

Prices of securities rises a bit

For this one, we are going to look at what you can do if the price of the chosen security goes up a little bit. There are a few strategies that can do well here, including the bull call spread, the bull put spread and the short put. The bull call spread can work out nicely because you will be able to use it to lower your upfront costs. However, this one is going to put some limitations on the profits that you earn if the asset rises too much.

The bull put spread is similar, but you will write the puts on the asset while also purchasing this number of puts. The nice thing about using this one is that you can earn a profit, even if the asset does not go up during your expiration date. However, if the asset doesn't rise at all during your time frame, or the increase is not very large during that time, then you will not be able to earn a ton of money in profits.

The short put is another strategy that you can work with during these market conditions. This is simply a sell to open order where you will write the puts on the asset you think will see an increase in price. To see success with this strategy, you will need to write close to the money put options that will expire pretty soon. With this kind of strategy, you will get the benefit of a simple strategy, but if your asset ends up going down in price, you can lose that money as well.

Prices of securities fall a bit

If you are watching the market, and you see that the prices of an asset are likely to fall down a bit, then there are three strategies that can help you to still make money on this asset. Picking out either the bear put spread, the bear call spread, or the short call can help you to earn an income in a falling market. With the bear put spread, you will have an advantage of having cheaper options when compared to gong with a put, but there will be a bit of limitation on the profits if your security falls a lot, rather than just a little bit.

Some investors will choose to work with the bear call spread with this market condition. With this one, you are going to write out the calls, and then you will purchase calls that have the same asset and the same expiry, but the ones that you purchase will have a strike price that is higher. This is a strategy that is usually reserved for advanced investors because it can be more difficult to handle. If you see that your asset falls a lot during your expiry time, your profits will be more limited. However, if the security stays steady and doesn't move down, you can still make a profit with this strategy.

And finally, you can work with what is known as the short call. This means that the trader is going to write out their call options either at or near the money. Ideally, to see this strategy to work, you need an expiry date that will be soon. When you use this strategy, even if the asset doesn't move, you can get a good profit. However, if the price goes down quite a bit, you can receive a loss of profit.

The price of the security goes up a lot

As an investor, if you think that the security is going to see a huge increase in its value in the near future, there are a few strategies that can help you to capitalize on this. These strategies include the long call and the short bull ratio spread. For the long call, you simply need to purchase an open order to purchase calls. The advantage of the long call is that you can potentially have limitless profits as long as the price does go up quite a bit within your expiration date. However, if your chosen security ends up not changing its price or the value goes down, there aren't any protections in place to save you.

You can also go with the bull ratio spread. This one is often saved for those investors who have been in the market for a long time. When using this strategy, it is important for you to purchase both write and buy calls of the same asset and these calls need to expire at the same time. You must make sure that you purchase more options than you write. The biggest advantage of this is that you will be putting protections in if the price of the asset starts to fall, or if it doesn't end up moving at all. This one doesn't provide you with limitless profits like the other one, though.

The price of the security goes down a lot

If you are working with a security and you think that the price is going to go down quite a bit, it is possible to work on a long put or a short bear ratio spread to help you out. The long put is pretty simple, and it is a good option for beginners. To start with this, you would need to work with your broker to use a buy to open order and then you would buy a put option on your asset. It is always best to buy at the money contracts, which basically means that the strike price is going to be the same as the market price. This helps you to keep a better handle on the risk that is going to be involved. If you feel that the security will fall soon, you can pick out a contract that has a close expiration date. The downside to this option is that if the price ends up rising or doesn't move during your time, you will not get the protection you need to cut your losses.

You can also work with is the short bear ratio spread. This one is going to be a bit complex, but it can help you so much. You will need to put puts and write puts at the same time, using the same asset and an identical expiry date. However, the written puts need to come in at a strike price that is higher. You also need to purchase more contracts than you will sell with this strategy. This is to help protect you if the asset stays constant or goes up. This sometimes results in lower profits, but it can protect your losses.

The security can go either up or down

Sometimes the market is so volatile that it is going to be difficult to figure out which way you should invest. You may be fairly sure that it will go one way, but you are uncertain because of how the market has been behaving lately. Th strategies that you can work on for this situation include the long straddle, the long strangle, the butterfly spread, and the long gut.

Many beginners will work with a long straddle in this situation because it increases your potential profit. You do need a big price change in your asset or you will end up with some losses. The long strangle, on the other hand, is cheaper than the long straddle, but you need to have a bigger change in your asset for you to make a profit.

Another option is to work with the long gut. This is a good strategy for a beginner because it involves buying what are known as in the money call options, while also being able to purchase the money put options. With all the purchases that you do, you should end up with the same expiration date and there should be an equal amount of put and call options when everything is done. If you look at the market and see that it will move soon, you should pick out options that provide you with shorter expiration dates.

The price of the security will not change

With this final option, we are going to look at what you can do if the asset you choose is not going to move at all. There are a few strategies that you can pick from when you think the asset price will stay the same. These include the short straddle, the short strangle, and the butterfly spread.

With the short straddle, you are dealing with what is known as a higher level of trading because you will need to use a sell to open your order. This allows you to write at the money calls. You also need to do this with the same amount of puts on the asset. You need the calls and puts to end on the same date, or at least as close as possible.

You can also work with the short strangle. To do this, you are responsible for writing call options and then the same amount of put options. These calls and puts need to be out of the money. If you are picking out contracts that are out of the money, the price of the asset will need to have a really large movement before you see a loss, so this makes them safer to use. In addition, you can reduce your risk a little bit by picking out an expiration date that is shorter-term.

It is not common for a beginner to go with a butterfly spread on this market condition because it is really hard to work with and costs more than some other strategies.

It does work and can help you to earn profits so you can certainly give it a try.

As you can see, there are many different market conditions that you can encounter when you are working with the options market. Understanding which strategies that you can use in different market conditions can help to expand out your profits and makes it possible to trade no matter what is going on in the market.

Specific strategies to try

We have now spent some time talking about how to react to different market conditions, but we have not looked specifically at any of the different strategies and how they work. Some of the different trading strategies that work great for the options market include:

- Covered call: The covered call strategy is going to require the investor to go in and purchase their asset. When you own this asset, you can then write a call option on them. This strategy will work well when a trader is trying to earn some profits from the call premium, while still protecting the investor in case the asset starts to lose some value. If the volatility increases with this strategy, the trader may end up losing. If the volatility decreases, you stand to gain more profit.

- Naked call: If you are looking for a riskier strategy in the options market, this is one to work with. The naked call is when the investor will sell their call option on an open market, but they don't technically own the asset. If the trade doesn't work the way that you planned, you end up losing a lot of money. On the other hand, when things work out well on the market, you can stand to gain a lot as well.

- Married put: The married put takes some time to learn because you end up doing a combination of the two strategies we talked about above. With this strategy, the investor will purchase the asset that they wish to use. At the same time, they will place a put option on them. This is a good strategy for a beginner because it can help protect them against short-term losses that they may incur.

- A bull call spread: The bull call spread is another choice to make. With this strategy, the trader will be able to purchase call options after a specific strike price is reached. When that strike price goes up a little bit, the trader will turn around to sell the option, making a profit on the difference that occurs. This is one that you will want to work with if you think the asset is about to go up in the near future.

- Bear put spread: The bear put spread is similar to the bull call spread, but it goes in the opposite direction with the market. With this one, you will purchase a put option rather than a strike price. When the strike price goes even lower, you will sell your option. You will want to work with this strategy any time that you think the price of your asset is likely to go down. As long as the price does go down, you will be able to make a profit.

- Protective collar: For the protective collar, you will need to purchase what is known as an out of the money put option. At the same time, you will also write an out of the money call option. This is a good strategy to use if the investor sees that the long position they are working with is doing well. The protective collar is good because it allows the trader to lock in the profits that they are getting without needing to sell the shares at the time.

- Long straddle: the long straddle is similar to the protective collar, but there are a few things you can change that make it unique. One difference is that while your put and call options will be for the exact same asset (and will use the same expiry date), they must have different strike prices. The price that is used with the call option needs to be higher than the put strike price, but both should still be out of the money. Some people like this better because it is less expensive, but it is a good strategy when you believe that the price of your asset is about to go up or down soon.

- Butterfly spread: The butterfly spread is going to be a combination of a few other strategies, so it can be nice if you are in a market that could use the bear spread and the bull spread at the same time. For this, you will need to purchase a call option at a low strike price. At the same time, you will sell two of your call options at a strike price that is higher. You can also choose to sell another call option at a higher strike price when compared to your other calls.

- Iron Condor: With the iron condor, the investor is going to hold onto a long position and a short position at the same time, but you need to make sure that your strangles are separate. This one works the best because you will be able to get started with selling your options since it won't result in a loss on both sides. Since you get to win on one side and only possibly lose on the other, this is a great way to learn the market and still make money.

As you can see, there are many different types of strategies that you can choose to work with. Some are going to be easier to work with and others may work the best when you are dealing with specific market conditions. Learning how to use a few of these strategies, and when these strategies will be the most effective, can make a difference on whether you will be successful when trading in the options market.

CHAPTER 5

COMMON TRADING MISTAKES

As a beginner, there are a lot of mistakes that you can make. You may go into options trading with a lot of good intentions, but without the proper knowledge, or taking time to really consider the positions that you are taking in options, it is easy to make mistakes and lose money. Options can be a good way to make some money, but many beginners will become confused and not understand what they are doing. In this chapter, we are going to take a look at some of the common mistakes that many beginners make when they enter the options market and the things that you can do to avoid these mistakes.

Not knowing the market

While you may think that working in options is not going to be that hard, the options market can be quite complex. Jumping in just because you read the definition of options or because someone else who made money in this market can be a really bad mistake. While there are some investors who believe that options are easier to work with compared to other investments, but getting too excited will lead you to make poor decisions that will take all your money on a bad trade.

It is important that you really learn about the options market before you decide to join in. Learning a few strategies, without fully understanding them, and joining the market just because it seems easy will just lead you to failure. Options trading is not all that simple and as you get into the market, you will find that there are many risks that come with it. The best thing that you can do to avoid these risks is to learn about this investment choice fully and then decide if it is right for you.

Never switching up your strategy

The way that you invest in options is going to depend on the market that you are dealing with. You will need to mix and match your strategies so they go along with the market. With other types of investments, you may have been told to pick one strategy and stick with it for the long-term. This allowed you to really learn the strategy and do well with it. But you will find that things are different when you work with options trading.

While it is advisable that you work with one strategy for the duration of a particular trade, it is not smart to only consider one strategy for each and every trade that you do. As the market changes, and as the asset that you are investing in changes, you will want to change up the strategy that you are working on as well.

It won't take you much time working in the options market to realize that one strategy all the time is not going to make you earn money. You need to be able to adjust based on the market you are working with, how volatile this market is, and more. If you don't like the idea of always learning a new strategy and switching things up, then options trading is not the best investment for you.

Not having an exit plan

For anyone who has ever worked with investments of any kind, especially those who have lost a significant amount of money, you know how important it can be to have an exit plan. Before you enter into a new trade, it is a good idea to have an exit plan in place. Write out this exit plan and stick with it. Be prepared to use this exit plan if the trade is not going the right way for you. This is one of the best ways to reduce the risks that you have in options trading. Without a good exit plan, you increase your risks of losing all your profits if you earned any, and your losses will grow quickly.

As an investor in options, it is always best to play it as safe as possible. You may not like the idea of getting out of the market early because it will cut into some potential profits, but it at least allows you the chance to gain some profit. And it is much better than staying inside the market more with the result of losing money.

There are three main ways that you are able to plan out the exit that you want to use. For the first one, you will set a time limit. With this, you may decide after a few months or so that you are going to exit the market, no matter what is going on. Some will choose to work on a target profit, where they are able to leave the market once they earn a specified amount of profit off that trade. And the third option is known as the technical exit. This means that you are going to leave the market when the security starts to do something like stalls or you see a fall in the prices.

Not working with a trading plan

As a beginner trader, one of the absolute worst things that you can do is to not put a plan in place right from the beginning. Without a good plan, how will you decide which options are the safest to work with, when you should get into and out of the market, and basically how to make your money? Without this plan, you will make decisions at the last minute when you are already in the market, without research and sound thinking to back them up, and it becomes almost impossible to earn the profits that you want.

Many people who enter the market without this good plan in place will go way beyond the boundaries that they set for themselves, and this means they will take on way more risk. With this option, you will run out of money really quickly. It is even possible to run out of money after just one trade. Before you even think about joining the market, even on your first trade, it is worth your time to set up a plan and stick with it to help prevent some of your losses.

Using revenge trading

No matter how prepared you are for options trading, there are going to be times when you receive a loss. Even the most experienced traders will have this happen to them. But when you receive a loss, you need to just learn from the mistake and move on to your next trade like it didn't happen. This is hard for people to do and sometimes, without thinking the decision through, they will decide to take on more and more risk in the hopes of earning some of that money back.

The problem with this is that it doesn't really work out. You are basically letting your emotions into the game and adding on more risk, without sound and thought out decisions, so you will make more mistakes. Once you get to this point and your emotions are taking over, you may as well leave the game altogether because your losses are just going to get bigger.

Working with out of the money option too much

There are some beginners who do not understand the options market well and who will focus most of their time on out of the money puts and calls. They often like this choice because these options are cheaper than the others. This is a mistake that even more, advanced traders can make because they work in other investments and are used to the idea of buying low and selling high. However, one of the best ways to make consistent money in the options market, you will find that OTMs aren't always the best strategy to go with.

This option may sound good on paper, but it can sometimes make it difficult for the investor to earn a profit. This is because for the investor to earn their money back, the asset price must be able to move above or below the strike price. And there is an expiration date that this movement must occur during. The move also needs to be big enough, either above or below, so that you can offset how much you will pay for the option. A lot of parts need to come together for the OTM to work, which shows how it is not always the best choice for you.

Picking out time frames that don't work

When it comes to options, an investor is going to find that timing can be very important. Some beginners will make mistakes when they start and they may pick out bad time frames or expiration dates. This means that they end up paying more on the option in order to prolong the time frame, or they may try to save themselves some money by picking out a time frame that is too short for what they need.

While considering the price is important when it comes to options, you also need to consider what the market is going to do in between the purchase and your expiration date. Some trades will obviously need more time, and some will be fine with the shorter time frame. Understanding how much time you will need can help you to only spend the amount that is necessary on each of your options.

Working with a bad broker

When you get into any type of investment, you will meet many brokers who are ready to help you out. There are a lot of brokers who know how to do their jobs and who can help you to make some money in options, and in other investments, in no time. But, there are also many brokers who are not that great, and some of them will end up being scam artists who just want to take your money.

If you are working with a full-service broker, someone who helps you out by giving advice and completing the trades for you, then it is important that you are selective about who you chose. Many brokers want to help you out, but some are more worried about what will make them the most money. Take a look at who you are working with, how much they cost, and how they will get paid when working with them to help you make the right decision. You should always check the motives behind each broker before you decide to work with them.

As a beginner, there is a lot to take in when it comes to working with options and the whole market can be confusing. Make sure to take a look at some of these common mistakes and learn what you can do to avoid them so that you don't end up losing money or dealing with other issues while working in the options market.

CHAPTER 6

EASY STEPS TO REDUCE YOUR RISKS

As an investor, you likely want to find the best ways to reduce your risks when it comes to options. While the potential profit may look good on paper, if the risk is too high, you will end up losing more money than you make in the market. There are some investments that provide less risk than others. For example, putting your money into a savings account and letting it accrue interest is relatively risk-free, but you will hardly make any money from this choice. There are some choices that are way riskier, but with these, you probably won't make any money at all.

Options trading can be risky. You are working with the stock market and if you don't take care and do your research and protect your investment, you could lose out on everything. The good news is that if you take care of your investment, there are things that you can do that will help you to reduce your risks and make it more likely that you will earn money. Let's take a look at some of the best tricks that you can do to help reduce your risks as a beginner so you can actually make money.

Create a plan

The first thing that you need to do when starting in options is to come up with a good plan of action and then write it down. It is tempting to spend a few minutes looking at the market and then jumping in. You may say that the plan is to make as much money as you can. But this is not a solid investment plan and will lead you to lose money. This kind of plan doesn't provide you with an enter or exit strategy, no investment strategy about how you will behave in the market, and nothing is planned out. You are basically winging it and hoping that things will work out. This rarely works out in the long run and you will end up losing a lot of money.

When creating your own plan, you need to add in as many details as possible. The first thing to list out is how much money you are hoping to make on your trades. Make this number be realistic. You will not make millions of dollars in options in your first year, but you can expect a tidy profit if you know what you are doing. While creating the plan, make sure to write down some other requirements, such as what needs to happen before you purchase an option and when you will leave the market once you enter.

This plan also needs to include which strategy you are planning on using. You can find many strategies that work well with options trading and it often depends on the options you want to work with and the type of market that is occurring. You aren't stuck with the same strategy all the time and many investors can find success when they mix up their strategies to fit the market conditions. This is why it is so important to learn a variety of strategies in the beginning. This can help you to pick out good options and make money, even when the market conditions change.

At some point, you are going to need to exit the market, even with options. Creating an exit strategy from the beginning can help you out. Before you enter into any trade, you need to determine the amount that you are comfortable with losing as well as what other conditions need to happen for you to leave a particular trade. Without putting this information in the plan, you will often stay in the market too long and end up losing a lot of money. Some investors can find it hard to leave the market, especially when they are doing well, but staying in too long can make you lose a lot of money. Setting up your exit strategy, in the beginning, can be so important for reducing the amount of risk that you are going to face.

There may seem like there are a lot of different parts that have to come together in your plan before you can even get into a trade, but having this information in place is so great for helping you out. It helps you to make the right decisions every step of the way, helps you to know what your goals are, and really can direct the decisions that you make with trading so you don't wing it at all. If you are confused on where you should be going with your trades or if you have a good plan in place, make sure to talk to your broker. They have worked with many kinds of traders in the past and they will be able to offer you some advice and help you write out that plan if you need it.

Don't forget the research

There are many people who hear about options and want to jump right in. They hear that options are a great way to make money and that they can even use leverage to put more down on bigger trades than what they have in their accounts. They may have heard stories about how someone was able to make a fortune overnight with options and they want to do the same thing. Yes, you are able to make good money when working on options, but it does take some work and there are some risks to doing it.

If you want to get into options trading and make money, you must be able to do your research. You have to spend time learning about the market so you can understand the best time to join and you can pick out the best strategies to make money. You need to learn what options are and how they work. You can listen to some of the experts in the field and learn what advice they are giving out. These are just a few of the things that you can research to help you see success with options.

Keep the emotions away

If you have ever looked at an investment, you have probably heard how you need to base all your decisions on facts, rather than your emotions. Once you start letting your emotions get the best of you during trading, you are going to start losing money. It doesn't matter what plan you had when you entered the trade or how well you may have done with your options ahead of time. Emotions cloud your judgment and it becomes really hard to stick with the good decisions that are needed for the options market. It is possible for every trader to become emotional, no one wants to lose a lot of money on a trade, but the good traders know how to stick with their plan and how to keep the emotions out of the decision-making process.

For those who are real emotions, or who know they will have trouble sticking with the plan they make because of their gains or losses in the market, then options trading is not the best investment for you. Investing in options can become really emotional and you have to have the right mindset to make this happen. Knowing your own emotional state and sticking with your original trading plan can make all the difference in how well you will do.

Ask your broker if they offer special features

You may not think that the broker is going to be that important. But the broker can provide you with a wealth of advice and extra help in the market. Not only are they able to help you make some of your trades and offer advice when you ask, there are some other special features that your broker may be able to offer, depending on who you chose.

The first feature that you should ask your broker about is a process that is known as an out of money rate. One issue that some beginners will come across when they are working with options is that they can lose on all of their initial investment. With the out of money rate, you have the possibility of getting some of this money back.

When you are using the out of money feature, you will enter into an agreement with the broker. If the broker offers this, they will return a small percentage of the investment that you put in if things don't go well on a trade. This is usually going to be about ten percent of the total investment. Not all brokers will offer this. The ones who do will often offer it just on your first few trades, but they see it as a way to help out their beginners and get the investors to stay around. This can benefit you as you get used to the market and will prevent you from losing out on everything.

Another feature that you can ask your broker about is the sell back feature. This is a feature that you can utilize if you are in a trade and you notice that one of the calls that you made is going badly and you think you will lose money. With the help of this feature, our broker gives you the opportunity to exit out of your trade ahead of the expiration time. When you leave your trade at an early time, you will need to forfeit some of your initial investment, usually up to sixty percent, but this can be a better option than losing all of your money.

Using the straddle strategy

One strategy that works really well for beginners who are getting started in options trading is known as the straddle strategy. When an asset has a lot of movement (also known as being volatile), it can be really bad for the trade depending on how fast the market moves and what predictions you made. When you use the straddle strategy, you are heading your bets. This is because you will use one asset and then put both a put and a call option on that asset.

This can work because it doesn't matter as much which way your asset ends up moving. You are putting a call and a put on that asset, so no matter which way the asset moves in the market, you will end up being right. Depending on which one is wrong and by how much, you do stand to risk some money, but you are more likely to win with this option than not. It is a good idea as a beginner to learn how to work with the straddle strategy early on to make the most money, with the least amount of risk, possible.

Manage the money you are using

You must be in complete control when it comes to using your money in options trading. This is one of the easiest ways for you to minimize how much money you are losing in the market. If you are someone who is in a lot of debt and can't seem to manage your money at all in real life, then it is not the best idea for you to work in the options money. You have to know where your money is and how to manage that money the whole time if you would like to be successful with this investment.

To manage your money, you need to create that trading plan that we talked about earlier. This plan needs to be done before you get started on the first trade. In addition, you must understand that sometimes the market is not going to behave the way that you want and there will be times when you will lose money. Even professional investors run into issues with losing money at times when the market doesn't behave the way that they want. Sometimes this is going to be one loss, and other times you may deal with a series of losses.

Now, you can choose to keep going the same way and hoping that things change around for you. Or you can manage your money and see if there are things that you can change up to prevent the losses. If you keep on with the series of losses, it is your own fault if you keep on losing into the future. At all times you need to know how much money you are investing, how your money is doing, and how much you stand to lose on each trade. If you stop paying attention to these numbers, it is not going to take long before all your money is gone.

Now that you know that it is possible that you may lose some money, you will be able to control how much you lose. You can add in an exit strategy to your plan, for example, that will tell you that you must stop trading once you have lost a certain amount of money. Or once you reach a win/loss ratio (that you set up before you started trading), you will decide to take a break from trading and regroup for a bit. Having these plans in place from the beginning will make such a big difference in when you lose money and how much, which is a huge determinant of how much risk you are taking on.

CONCLUSION

Thank you for making it through to the end of this book, let's hope it was informative and able to provide you with all of the tools you need to achieve your goals whatever they may be.

The next step is to decide if options trading is the right choice for you. There are many different types of investments that you can work with, but this guidebook spent some time looking at options trading and all the great things that you can do to turn this investment into an income stream.

This guidebook spent some time talking about options and how they work. Even as a beginner, you will be able to use some of the strategies and tips in this guidebook to help you to earn money without needing a lot of money down to help you get started.

When you are looking to get started with investments, or you would like to expand out your portfolio, options trading can be the best choice for you to make. This guidebook will provide you with all the information that you need to get started with earning a good return on investment with options.

Finally, if you found this book useful in any way, a review on Amazon is always appreciated!

If you want you can subscribe to our newsletter: http://bit.ly/2EZWzlJ

www.ingramcontent.com/pod-product-compliance
Lightning Source LLC
Chambersburg PA
CBHW071230220526
45468CB00002B/790